Ocean Animals

Stingrays

by Christina Leaf

BELLWETHER MEDIA
MINNEAPOLIS, MN

Blastoff! Beginners are developed by literacy experts and educators to meet the needs of early readers. These engaging informational texts support young children as they begin reading about their world. Through simple language and high frequency words paired with crisp, colorful photos, Blastoff! Beginners launch young readers into the universe of independent reading.

Blastoff! Universe

Reading Level

Grade K

Grades 1-3

Grade 4

Sight Words in This Book 🔍

a	has	like	some	what
and	have	long	the	
are	here	look	their	
can	in	many	there	
eat	is	on	they	
for	it	sit	to	

This edition first published in 2021 by Bellwether Media, Inc.

No part of this publication may be reproduced in whole or in part without written permission of the publisher. For information regarding permission, write to Bellwether Media, Inc., Attention: Permissions Department, 6012 Blue Circle Drive, Minnetonka, MN 55343.

Library of Congress Cataloging-in-Publication Data

Names: Leaf, Christina, author.
Title: Stingrays / by Christina Leaf.
Description: Minneapolis, MN : Bellwether Media, 2021. | Series: Blastoff! beginners: ocean animals | Includes bibliographical references and index. | Audience: Ages PreK-2 | Audience: Grades K-1
Identifiers: LCCN 2020032012 (print) | LCCN 2020032013 (ebook) | ISBN 9781644873984 (library binding) | ISBN 9781648340758 (ebook)
Subjects: LCSH: Stingrays--Juvenile literature.
Classification: LCC QL638.8 .L43 2021 (print) | LCC QL638.8 (ebook) | DDC 597.3/5--dc23
LC record available at https://lccn.loc.gov/2020032012
LC ebook record available at https://lccn.loc.gov/2020032013

Editor: Amy McDonald   Designer: Andrea Schneider

Printed in the United States of America, North Mankato, MN.

Table of Contents

Stingrays!   4
Body Parts   8
On the Move   14
Stingray Facts   22
Glossary   23
To Learn More   24
Index   24

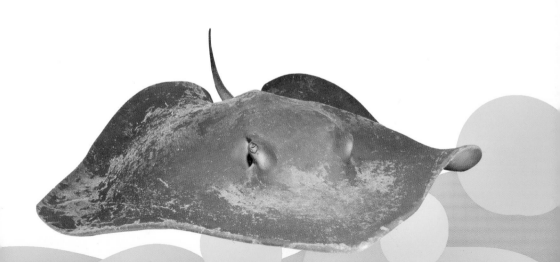

Stingrays!

What is in
the sand?
A stingray!

Stingrays are
flat fish.
There are
many kinds.

blue-spotted
ribbontail ray

southern
stingray

yellow
stingray

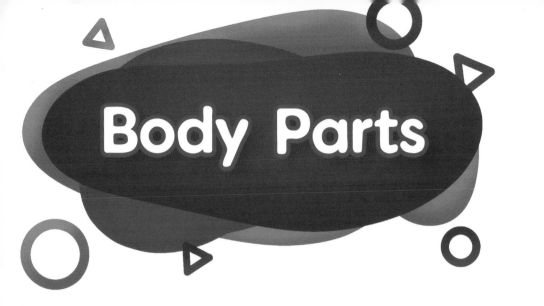

Body Parts

A stingray
has a long tail.
It has a
sharp **spine**.

spine

tail

It has a flat body.
Its eyes sit on top.

eyes

Look below!
Here are its
mouth and **gills**.

gills

mouth

On the Move

Many stingrays move like a wave. Some flap their **fins**.

fins

They look
for food.
They eat clams
and crabs.

clams

They hide
to stay safe.
They lie
in the sand.

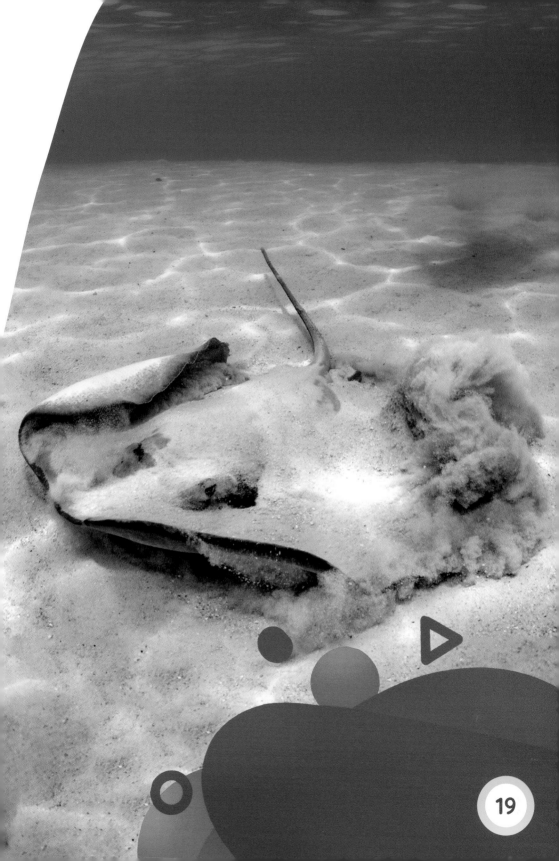

Stingrays
can hurt!
Their spines
have **venom**.
Ouch!

Stingray Facts

Stingray Body Parts

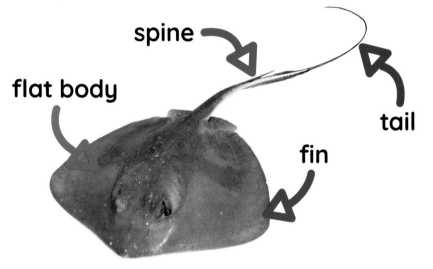

spine

flat body

tail

fin

Stingray Food

clams   crabs   shrimp

Glossary

fins

thin body parts
that stick out

gills

body parts that
help fish breathe

spine

a sharp part on
a stingray's tail

venom

a poison that
hurts animals

To Learn More

ON THE WEB

FACTSURFER

Factsurfer.com gives you a safe, fun way to find more information.

1. Go to www.factsurfer.com.

2. Enter "stingrays" into the search box and click Q.

3. Select your book cover to see a list of related content.

Index

body, 10
clams, 16
crabs, 16
eyes, 10
fins, 14, 15
fish, 6
food, 16
gills, 12, 13
hide, 18
kinds, 6
mouth, 12, 13
move, 14
safe, 18
sand, 4, 18
spine, 8, 20
tail, 8, 9
venom, 20